Strong Beautiful African American Women

Melvin C. Ryan

All Rights Reserved. No part of this work may be used or reproduced in any manner whatsoever without written permission from the author except in the case of brief quotation embodied in articles or reviews

ISBN-13: 978-0692683804
(Melvin C. Ryan)

ISBN-10: 0692683801

Cover designed by: Melvin C. Ryan and Paul D. Holmes

Cover photograph: Mrs. Leontine Chatman – Mother (left); Mrs. Elizabeth Williams – Maternal Grandmother (right) taken in 1943 in 2600 block of Washington Blvd, Chicago, IL

Edited by: Shawn C. Kennedy

Book Printed in the United States of America

©2016 Melvin C. Ryan

To Honor All

Strong
Beautiful
African American
Women

DEDICATION

To Paul D. Holmes, my best friend, whose encouragement, loyalty and insistence helped me to improve my mind, grow intellectually and broaden my scope. You see, because of my advanced years, I had almost given up hope. But because of his unyielding support, this work came into fruition. Beautiful Black women, strong as a large oak tree – you are like the Rock of Gibraltar to me.

Your arms like the eagle's wings spread wide as the sea to embrace young boys, girls, and even men like me...

Contents

INTRODUCTION 1
ACKNOWLEDGMENTS 3

WOMEN 7

THANK YOU 9
FORGIVE ME 10
LEAST WE FORGET 12
BEAUTIFUL BLACK QUEEN 15
LOVE THE SISTERS 17
MA' STUFF 18
MASA'S DEMISE 19
FREEDOM 20
BEAUTIFUL BLACK WOMEN 22
SET ME FREE 24
TRUE LOVE 26
MY BEAUTIFUL ROSE 27
MOTHER AND SON 29
WAS GOOD TO MY WOMAN 30
OUT OF THE NEST 31
QUEEN OF THE UNIVERSE 32
BEAUTIFUL BLACK PEARL 33
I'VE TRIED SO HARD 35
MOTHER'S GRIEF 36
GET SMART 37

MY BEAUTIFUL BLACK PRINCESS 38
THE MASTER NARRATIVE................................... 40
WHY BE FOOLISH... 42
NATIONAL COUNCIL OF NEGRO WOMEN 45
MRS. MARY MCLEOD BETHUNE......................... 48

EDUCATION 51

SACRED HEART SCHOOL...................................... 53
PASSING THE TORCH 56
THE PROJECTS 57
THE OKIE DOKE 58
RUNNING OUT OF TIME 60
UNITE 61
JESUS AND BOOKS... 62
BACK TO THE PAST... 64
ATTITUDE.. 65
EDUCATION IS THE WAY...................................... 66
RUN MOVE 67

REFLECTIONS 69

SAVE THE CHILDREN 70
NO BED OF ROSES.. 71
STAND UP, BE COUNTED...................................... 72
STRENGTH.. 74
THE DEMISE OF THE POWERFUL...................... 75
MISGUIDED... 76

WORK 78
VIOLENCE ON TV 79
KINDRED SPIRITS 80
CHRISTMAS IS 81
NO NAME 82

SELF-ESTEEM 85

IT IS US AGAINST THE WORLD 86
THE MASTER PLAN 87
THE DOPE FIEND SCROOGE 88
STOP! WAKE UP 91
TOO GOOD FOR DOPE 92
HAVE A PURPOSE 96
BLACK GENOCIDE 97
HONOR 98
THINK 100
SHAME 101
YOU THINK YOU'RE GREAT 102
BRING BACK SANITY 103
LOVE 105
LOVE AND RESPECT 106
TRY JESUS 107
WHAT DO WE NEED? 109
JESUS MY MOTIVATOR 110
FAMILY AGAIN 113
TOGETHERNESS 114
SURVIVAL 115
MY OWN SALVATION 117
A HOUSE DIVIDED 118

MY NEIGHBORHOOD 119
DR. KING 120

INTOLERANCE 123

BE KIND 124
IS THIS TRUE? 125
BLACK FACE 128
JUST TO FEEL FREE 130
THE MASON 131
THEY DIDN'T GET TO KNOW ME 134
GOD'S CHILDREN 135
UNHONORED 136
DON'T BLAME ME 139
THE TRUTH WILL SET YOU FREE 140
WE ARE IN THIS TOGETHER 141
NORTH OF THE MASON DIXON LINE 142
OTHER 143

PRAYER 145

TRY PRAYER 146
OUR SURVIVAL IS IN THEE 147
WILL IT EVER END? 149
HELP 151
LOOKING FOR A SMILE 152
FAITH 153
JESUS IS NEAR 154

COME TOGETHER 155

MONOLOGUES 157

AMERICA, I LOVE YOU! 158
THE BENCH.. 167
GOD'S JUDGMENT OR MAN PLAYING GOD? 179
I AM MAD AS CAN BE 185
ALL WE HAVE LOST AND WHERE DID IT GO?
.... 189

TABLE OF PHOTOGRAPHS
of
Strong, Beautiful African American Women

MRS. ELIZABETH ROBINSON LINTON, WILLIAMS 8
MRS. KATE HARVEY RYAN 16
MRS. LEONTINE LINTON GUIDRY, CHATMAN 23
MRS. ANNIE MAE BREAUX RIOUS 28
MRS. DOROTHY AMANDA PORTER HOLMES 34
MRS. LENORA RYAN WILSON 39
MRS. MATILDA BREAUX REDFUD 44
MRS. MINNIE LEE BUXTON RYAN 50
MS. MARY "TULA" RYAN 52
MRS. PEARL RYAN MOLESS 52
MS. ELNORA FIGARO 52
MRS. MARGIE HAFLER HOLMES 55
MRS. LILLIAN RYAN JOHNSON, WOODARD 59
MRS. IVORY ROCHON HONORÉ 63
MRS. DOROTHY HOLMES CLARK 68
MRS. LUCILLE DAVIS 73
MRS. STELLA "MOM" BREAUX 77
MRS. MARY HAILEY HARRIS 83
MRS. MARY ROBINSON BROWN 90
MRS. LUCILLE HOLMES GILES 95
MRS. LUCILLE CAROLINE MAURA HOLMES 99
MS. AIMEE OLIVE HOLMES 104
MRS. ALMA SMYLES CURTIS "MS LOVE" 108
MRS. DEBRA PRICE-RYAN 112
MRS. AMY GUIDRY ROCHON 116

MRS. SHIRLEY BUTTON HOLMES.................121
MS. EARNESTINE ANN PORTER..................127
MS. STELLA MAE BREAUX..........................133
MRS. IDELLA GRAY LANDRY..........................138
MRS. ELAINE WILTZ HOLMES........................144
LADIES OF LAKE CHARLES............................150
MRS. "SUGAR DOO"..150
MRS. AMY GUIDRY ROCHON..........................150
MRS. GIVENS..150
MRS. ALMA SMYLES CURTIS..........................150
MRS. BARKAY...150
MRS. HALEY..150
MRS. SUSIE WILLIAMS CASTILLE....................156
MRS. RUTH DIXON..166
THE BENCH..177
MRS. BEATRICE LAFLEUR GUIDRY..................178
MS. ELIZABETH CECELIA PORTER..................184
MRS. ELLA ROUGEAU LAFLEUR......................188

(Unless otherwise acknowledged photographs are from the Collection of Melvin C. Ryan)

FOREWORD

I always say you can tell a lot about a Black man's image of "self" simply by observing his interactions with women and listening to what he says about them in their absence. The relationships that men experience during our formative years with our mothers, grandmothers, great-grandmothers, aunts, and sisters—as well as with other African American women in our communities like our teachers, neighbors and mentors—are intricately woven into our emotional and spiritual make-up as men. These experiences directly influence the type of men, fathers, grandfathers, great-grandfathers, uncles, brothers, friends, lovers and mentors we will grow-up to become.

In his book titled ***Strong, Beautiful African American Women***, Melvin C. Ryan has masterfully conveyed the essence of the indomitable spirit, strength and perseverance that is innate within African American women and the profound respect he has for them. Through the powerful artistry of his written words, Melvin skillfully embeds images onto the minds of his readers, allowing them to subconsciously teleport back in time to various decades, in which to capture the embodiment of his relationships and interactions with strong, beautiful African American women. Melvin's penmanship is a true testament to his genuine admiration for African American women and is a conduit which reflects what he holds true to his heart.

I sometimes worry that many of our youths do not appear to have a structured and progressive direction in their lives. When this occurs, I become critical of our elders for not passing on the "real" history of our people to subsequent generations. Melvin's selected poetry, prose and monologues lay the tapestry of this history and remind us that African American women possesses royal beauty and a great level of determination and endurance. I only hope that both men and women, who partake in this written and visual journey with Melvin, benefit from his "old-school" wisdom, knowledge and experiences. You will gain a deeper understanding of "self", which in turn will positively influence how you treat and interact with others. It will also give you a better image of the great man Melvin grew up to become based on the many positive relationships he experienced with strong, beautiful African American women.

Shawn C. Kennedy
Chicago
March 07, 2016

INTRODUCTION

The idea for writing this book came from my personal experiences as a child growing up in Lake Charles, Louisiana during the Great Depression of the 1930s and 1940s and my teenage and adult experiences. I witnessed firsthand the joys, humiliations, hardships and struggles that women had to endure for their families. I wanted to recount what I experienced during this time period. I had this burning inside of me to write about the events I witnessed and those that were told to me by family and friends. Over the years, I took many notes and jotted down poems and ideas to develop. **Strong, Beautiful African American Women** is the culmination of all those years. Drawing from my knowledge of these events in my life, my writings cover the period of time from my childhood to the present. I chose the medium of poetry, prose and monologue to share my feelings and memories because each one expresses a different tone of genuine emotion. Photographs of some of the Beautiful, Strong African American Women, who through their nurturing or friendship, influenced my life and are included in this book. This work was many years in the making. It has given me a feeling of joy and achievement to put my experiences over the years into writing I hope the younger generations will gain knowledge of our past and take note of our experiences for their future.

ACKNOWLEDGMENTS

As we travel through this short journey called life, we encounter forces both positive and negative, which have great influences on our lives. I would like to acknowledge and thank the persons who contributed to my advancement. If by chance I should miss someone, believe me it was not intentional, so please do not take offense.

I would like to thank Paul D. Holmes for his unwavering support and love without which this work could not have been completed and Mr. Otis McClees for his assistance. Mrs. Lola Young-Pryce whose love and concern helped me get through many hungry days when I was a boy in elementary school. She was a great lady. Mrs. Blanche Williams-Hadnot, my third grade teacher. I shall never forget meeting her or how she influenced my young life in a most positive way. Thanks to the ladies who helped nurture and guide me while growing up in Lake Charles, and thanks to Mrs. Stella Breaux who accepted me as one of her family. Special thanks to Mrs. Alma Curtis, Mrs. Sarah Johnson, Mrs. Ella Mae Lewis, Ms. 'Sugar Doo', Mrs. Martha Williams, and Mrs. Viola Higginbottom. These ladies were there for me. I was friends with their children and I called these ladies "Mom" to. Ms. Stella Mae Breaux, Mrs. Mildred Breaux Jones, Mrs. Matilda Breaux Redfud, Mrs. Annie Mae Breaux Rious and Mrs. Susie Williams Castille were my "sisters" in Lake Charles. As a teenager growing up in Chicago, there were Mrs. Leola Bennett, Mrs. Lucille Davis, Aunt Amy Guidry and Aunt Waver Taylor Guidry and cousin Mrs. Ivory Rochon Honoré, whose guidance and love saw me through many phases of growing up in Chicago. These women, along with the women in the photographs infused in me the love, respect and moral values that have made me the man I am today. I would also like to thank Mrs. Derotha Rogers-Clay and Mr. Esters Greer for the gracious and friendly way they assisted me with this endeavor. Many thanks to Mrs. Woodard and Mr. Hamburg from Olive-Harvey College, and Dr. Stanciel, instructor of English at Kennedy-

King College. A special thanks to Mr. Shawn Kennedy for his editing skills.

Melvin C. Ryan

WOMEN

STRONG, BEAUTIFUL AFRICAN AMERICAN WOMEN

Mrs. Elizabeth Robinson Linton, Williams Maternal Grandmother

THANK YOU

How beautiful, strong, faithful,
devoted and fine you are, Black
women; you are one of a kind!

Thank you for your time
and all you did to help
me improve my mind.

FORGIVE ME

Black women, the Genesis of all mankind I come to you humbly, but proudly, to ask your forgiveness and understanding.

Forgive me for not being with you on cold wintry nights when you needed a strong man to hold you tightly and to let you know and give you the assurance that everything would be all right.

Forgive me for planting my seed in your warm garden of love and leaving you alone to raise the beautiful fruit in this jungle with only help from above.

Forgive me for not saying, "I'm sorry," when I hurt you and for not being true.

Forgive me for not fighting back when the white man felt your breast, patted your behind and back.

Women

Forgive me for being irresponsible for so
many years and for ignoring all of your tears.

Can you forgive me for not being true and for
refusing to say to the minister and you, "I do"?

If you can, before God and the world, I
promise you; I will be a better man.

LEAST WE FORGET

There have been times in our country, even when we were considered to be free, that it was open season on you and me.

Especially, Black women who worked for white men and were subjected to all kinds of indignities.

When in white peoples' homes standing at the stove cooking, or standing at the sink washing dishes, the man of the house and sometimes even his sons, would come behind her and feel her breast and behind.

She would stand there biting her lips as tears rolled down her cheeks.
When she really wanted to throw hot grease or boiling water on them.

But in those days, Black women had no one to turn to.

Women

If she complained, she could be fired and not get a job in that town again.

Better yet, if a white man or woman accused her of something, she was guilty; she had no rights when it came to a white person.
The Black woman, after suffering these indignities, was still subjected to more abuse from her Black husband who, too, was under great strain.

He could not defend himself from the white man, so he took out his frustrations on his children and wife.

Black women always stood by their men. Even when he was not working, he was the man in his home. And contrary to what you might hear, Black women did not emasculate the Black man. If she had to – as they say – wear the pants, they were not her husband's; they were hers.

So, my brothers, if you prefer to date or marry other women, that is your prerogative. But, for God's sake, please do not get in public and degrade your Black sisters.

Remember: when you do this, you are giving ammunition to the enemy to shoot us all down.

So, let's love, cherish, and protect the beautiful Black women.

They have earned it!

BEAUTIFUL BLACK QUEEN

Beautiful Black Queen, the loveliest flower I have ever seen; how wonderful it would be if I were permitted to bathe in your radiance and sip the nectar, rain, and dew from your petals.

You allure us with your beauty, and we are blinded by its brilliance. Enfold us in your branches, and let us enjoy the rapture of your caress, and let me melt in your tenderness.

STRONG, BEAUTIFUL AFRICAN AMERICAN WOMEN

Mrs. Kate Harvey Ryan
Paternal Grandmother

LOVE THE SISTERS

Say, brothers, why do you treat the sisters so bad? Man, it's really sad. Is this some kind of fad?

Learn your history. Don't you know the sister has never been free? Just like you and me, she has had her share of misery, and there have been times the man had her hanging from a tree.

Can't you see the man raped her in the field, out house, big house, then came you and me, and bastards they made us be? And if we looked at his woman, a lynching you would see.

So, let's love, respect, and protect our sisters.
Then we will all be happy and free.
Don't you see!

MA' STUFF

Ole Missus caught ole Marsa feeling my stuff, and she looked at me and said, "Damn it! I have had enough!"

And I say to myself, "Yeah sum, I know how you feels 'cause I done poison his grits, meal, and snuff. And he won't be bothering both of us."

MASA'S DEMISE

Lawd, have mercy: po ole masa dead.

Dat poison I done give him done gone to his head.

I hope da don't find the bottle I don hid under his bed.

FREEDOM

Fa years I toiled for ole marse;

I slaved in the hot sun, worked hard and prayed keeping my mind on the hereafter.

One day with my children, we run into the night fighting the rain, snakes and all animals in sight.

Hallelujah! The Underground Railroad would end our plight.

Thank God! We made it to the promise land into the light.

Then, one day the slave hunters came in sight to take us back to the plantation overnight.

I rushed to my children and yelled with all my might.

Women

Ole marse, you comin' after me, but I's gonna make sure my children dies free.

BEAUTIFUL BLACK WOMEN

Beautiful Black women, strong as a large oak tree – you are like the Rock of Gibraltar to me.

Your arms like the eagle's wings spread wide as the sea to embrace young boys, girls, and even men like me.

We wonder what we would be if we had not been able to stand under your wings and branches and to share in all the love, wisdom, protection and support that come from thee?

How wonderful it would be if you were put up front for the whole world to see!

Thank you for all you have done to save the boys, and girls, and black men like me.

Women

Mrs. Leontine Linton Guidry, Chatman
Mother

SET ME FREE

Beautiful Black women, please forgive me, and set me free from all of my pain and misery.

I have sinned against and wronged thee. Blind I was and could not see how wonderful and good you were to me.

You saw me through all the bad years and eased my fears.
You even dried my tears.
With real devotion
and very little emotion,
you helped me cross this vast ocean.

There were times when I wanted to give up. I said, "I can't take it." You said, "Keep pushing, baby; you can make it."

Make it I did; then I got the big head and almost blew my lid.
I no longer had time for you and the kids.
Then, I left the crib and hid.

I wanted to be free and find me.
So, you see: I got wild and didn't do what I ought… I had plenty of time – I thought.

Then, something told me; time is not your friend; it's your enemy.

Thank God my eyes finally opened, and in my mind eyes, for me, only you I could see.

God was good, kind, and gracious.   He sent you back to me.
Oh, how great it is for me to open my eyes and see and thank you for forgiving me and setting me free from all of my pain and misery!

TRUE LOVE

Talking about you: selfish and unkind...
Boy, you losing your mind?

Many times, I done spank your behind
to let you know I love you, and you is mine.

I'll kill you myself before I see the judge give
you some time.

MY BEAUTIFUL ROSE

Oh! My beautiful rose like a fly caught in the web of a spider; I am entrapped by your beauty and your fragrance.

Though the thorns on your branches may wound me, they are oblivious to me – you see, I am in paradise when I gaze upon your magnificent loveliness.

So, let us become one in love – though separate in spirit and thought; we can be entwined into each other's heart.

Mrs. Annie Mae Breaux Rious
(Curtesy of Mrs. Annie Rious)

MOTHER AND SON

My beautiful Black women, you have made it against great odds, even though at times life has dealt you a stacked deck of cards.

Some people say it can't be done, but you say, "Yes my son. The world is there for you to conquer it. Nothing can stop you. Everything is there for you and you can achieve. Only have faith, and trust in God, work hard and believe."

WAS GOOD TO MY WOMAN

I did more for my woman than you and her parents have done.

Yes, that's right, I said I did more for my woman than you and her parents ever done.

I bought her a house, fur coat, car, and some hair, cause you never gave her none.

OUT OF THE NEST

When I look at you, I see class falling and going downhill fast.

What a waste! You have lost all taste, and you have so much time to kill, and you have lost the will to be constructive and productive.

When I think of all the sacrifices that were made to help you get ahead – the best schools, and now, you walk the streets day and night; you would rather beg than work and try to get ahead.

It appears you are lost and it is said a rolling stone gathers no moss.

Well, I have one more bridge to cross, and that is like the mama bird: I must push you out of this nest, so I can get some rest.

QUEEN OF THE UNIVERSE

Black woman you are Queen of the Universe, and that makes you first.

You preceded everyone walking on this Earth.

You gave life to everyone that's here. Number one, you have always been, the DNA, the Master Key, all humans descended from thee.

Strong, reliable, nurturing, supporting, loving and free.
The world should acknowledge you!

BEAUTIFUL BLACK PEARL

My love, my beautiful Black Pearl; your absence has left a void and loneliness in my life.

I am desolate for your presence. Touch me once more; it appears I'm destine to be prostrate at your door.

Open your heart and let me in. I shall be your devoted lover and friend until the end.

STRONG, BEAUTIFUL AFRICAN AMERICAN WOMEN

Mrs. Dorothy Amanda Porter Holmes

I'VE TRIED SO HARD

You all wonder why I fuss.
Who can I trust?
And why do you cuss?
Trying to get you to mind,
it seems like a waste of time.
Are you losing your mind?

I tried to show you a better way.
Night and day I pray to keep you from going
astray.
But it seems no matter
how hard I try,
my words just fly
over your head and die.

Why can't I reach you? Can't you see?
If you circumvent the law, a payment is due,
and darling mama don't want to lose you.

MOTHER'S GRIEF

Look at your head. What a mess! Looks just
like a bird's nest.

Boy you are causing me so much stress.
How can I help you out of this mess?
You used to be my best
and brought me much happiness.
Where did I go wrong?

I gave you a good Christian home, and I never
left you alone.
Nobody is prone to be bad.
Sometimes I wish I had stayed with your dad.

Lord, it's really sad;
I gave all that I had.
Now, Lord, I put him in your hands.

I know you have plans.
Please help my son to become a good,
God-fearing man.

GET SMART

My young sisters, why do you treat yourselves so mean? Is it a lack of self-esteem? Don't let anyone rob you of your dreams.

If you must have a young man, make sure he is working, proud – not mean – and that he has a dream. And demand he treats you like a queen.

MY BEAUTIFUL BLACK PRINCESS

My beautiful black princess,
I am intoxicated by your beauty
Oh, sober me with your love;
Let me enjoy your tenderness,
Caress me and free my imprisoned heart
Oh, clear my thoughts and together
We can melt into each other's arms.
Though separate we maybe as the fingers on
the hand.

Together we can solidify our plans and hand in
hand we can fly, shoot to the sky.

Mrs. Lenora Ryan Wilson
(From Collection of Charles Ryan, Sr.)

THE MASTER NARRATIVE

The Master Narrative will never get the best of me; no Barbie doll or blue eyes do I need to set me free.

Bleach your skin; dye your hair; be ashamed of your nose, eyes, and lips. I am proud because the Lord gave me my fat thighs and wide hips.

So, make yourself over if you choose; I am proud of my Black eyes, wide nose, kinky hair.

You won't see me letting the Master Narrative have me singing the blues, and you won't hear me saying,

"I don't want Black men doing any work for me… I hire white men if I choose." Brothers and Sisters, with that kind of thinking we all lose. Sell your crack; buy your crack; smoke your pipe; run the streets, and prey upon your

Women

brothers and sisters in the night.
Fuss and fight; shoot our children; try to
destroy our babies, our young women and
men; steal from each other if you dare.

Oh, Lord! Is there something in the air that
causes us not to care?

My God, look how we act: shooting each other
in the back – Oh, Lord! Sometimes I think I am
going to crack.

Wake up! Stop these attacks. Don't let the
Klan, skinheads, Nazis and the Master
Narrative have us continuing these vile acts!

Stop these attacks, and bring some sanity back.

Stop running in packs.
Be proud to be Black.
Unity, love, and respect
is the best way to fight back!

WHY BE FOOLISH

I don't care what these doctors and their reports say about cholesterol, grease, and fat.

I am going to continue to eat what I want and use my lard because, honey, that's where it's at.

My grandma and grandpa lived for years, and they ate like that
– using that good fat back and didn't take any of those pills and worry about a heart attack.

They used garlic and vinegar to cure their ills and never had to shed any tears.

What you say, Doctor? I got to stop eating that pork; I done had a stroke. But there is still hope.

Lord, have mercy. Why was I such a dope?

Please see me through this, Jesus, and I won't eat any more of that pork – fried, salted, or smoked.

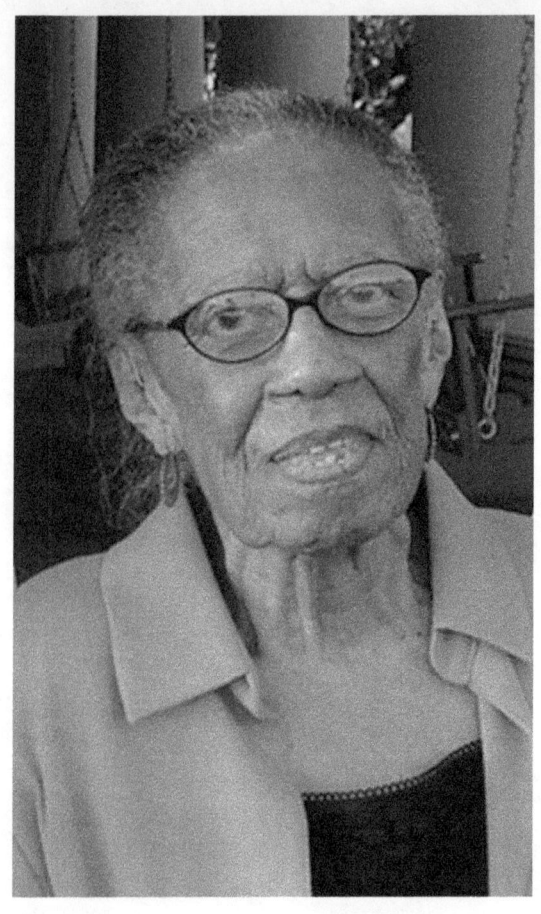

Mrs. Matilda Breaux Redfud
(From Collection of Mrs. Matilda Redfud)

NATIONAL COUNCIL OF NEGRO WOMEN
Dorothy Height

Most – if not all – Black women should belong to the National Council of Negro Women.

If you have a problem with the word NEGRO, think back in time, and see the kind of people we were when we were Negroes.

I salute all the wonderful Black women who were there to stand beside us, love us, and give us the strength we needed and still need.

African Americans are appealing for role models; if people knew their history, they would be familiar with all the wonderful Black women and men who laid the groundwork for African Americans.

Mrs. Mary McLeod Bethune, Mrs. Lola Young Pryce, Mrs. Fannie Lou Hamer, Mrs. Harriet Tubman, Mrs. Shirley Chisholm, Ms. Barbara Jordan, Mrs. Eleanor Holmes Norton, Mrs. Coretta Scott-King, Ms. Margaret Walker, Dr. Dorothy Height, Ms. C. Delores Tucker, Mrs. Marian Wright-Edelman, Ms. Lena Horne, Ms. Ella Fitzgerald, Ms. Cicely Tyson, Ms. Marian Anderson, Ms. Leontyne Price, our mothers, great-grandmothers, grandmothers, aunts, and school teachers are just a few of the great women who have helped to lay the groundwork.

Mrs. Mary McLeod Bethune heads the list. No one knows how many times her having conversations with Mrs. Roosevelt affected our lives in a most positive way.

So, in the memory of this great lady, and all of our great women, let us absent ourselves from the river boats, liquor stores, and dope dens even if it is only for one day a week, so we can keep our great organizations viable.

Ladies and gentlemen, the spirit of our Congress, Senate, and courts, both federal and state, should be sending us a wakeup call. Also with Mr. Newt Gingrich, Mr. Bob Dole, Mr. Phil Gramm, Judge Clarence Thomas, the Klan, skinheads, and militia groups snapping at our heels, we will need these organizations again. So, please let's do everything we can to support them.

As old Black ladies use to say, "Never forget the bridge that carried you across."

MRS. MARY MCLEOD BETHUNE

Mrs. Mary McLeod Bethune, a truly magnificent soul who left us too soon. A beautiful jewel was she: honest and bold with a heart as big as the sea.

Oh, how she fought for you and me. Strong as the Rock of Gibraltar was she.

A precious jewel: Her radiance was there for the whole world to see.

She walked the streets and sidewalks of the White House Grounds with pride and great dignity. Most times she was there for us, you see.

Learn your history, and keep this great lady in your memory.

I am sure the angels did rejoice when this great African American lady they did greet.

Women

Oh, what a day it must have been
when she knelt at Our Father's feet!

Mrs. Minnie Lee Buxton Ryan, Aunt
(From Collection of Charles Ryan, Sr.)

EDUCATION

STRONG, BEAUTIFUL AFRICAN AMERICAN WOMEN

Ms. Mary "Tula" Ryan   Mrs. Pearl Ryan Moless
Aunt   Aunt

Ms. Elnora Figaro, Cousin

Started the 1st Catholic School for Colored Children Sacred Heart in Lake Charles, Louisiana 1908

Education

SACRED HEART SCHOOL

In Lake Charles, Louisiana at Kaye Ryan's, home, (my great-grandfather), the first colored Catholic school Sacred Heart was founded in 1908, started by my cousin Ms. Eleanor Figaro, Aunt Pearl Ryan and Aunt Mary "Tula" Ryan. Colored gentlemen of Lake Charles came together and built the Little Red School House in 1910. My aunt Mary Ryan and cousin Eleanor Figaro were teachers and through their efforts Sacred Heart became the most important institution for black Catholics in Lake Charles.

Mother Katherine Drexel, (now Saint Katherine Drexel) founder, of the Sisters of the Blessed Sacrament came and built a new school in 1922. The school was staffed by the Sisters of the Blessed Sacrament which included both elementary and high school; Aunt Mary and cousin Eleanor remained as teachers. The Little Red School House was used until 1973 when it was turned into an early childhood center and was named the Eleanor Figaro Early Childhood Center. The high school remained in use until 1967; it closed because of lack of students due to integration.

Education

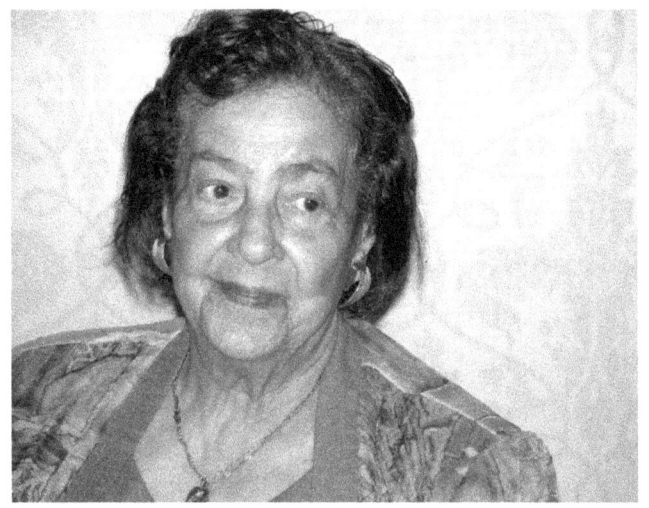

Mrs. Margie Hafler Holmes

PASSING THE TORCH

Our home environment, surroundings, parents, ministers, teachers, and friends are the things that decide our destiny and influence our lives.

If early in life we are given the love of God, self, parents and friends and are taught voracity, honesty, principle and integrity; we have the most important foundation to help us succeed in life. And when some loving hand lights the torch and passes it on to us with tender love, then our path will always be bright.

But, if we should neglect this light, and it flickers from lack of loving care, then there will be sorrow and shame to replace its flame… And we would cheat ourselves of fortune and fame.

THE PROJECTS

The projects, the concrete jungle, is the place I used to call home.

That is where the Vice-Lords, Disciples, Crips, and Bloods roam.

I am one of the lucky ones who was able to escape that cement and stone to find safety in another home.

When I look back and see the devastation, I thank God I got me an education.

THE OKIE DOKE

So, you say affirmative action is bad, and you are a young black conservative Republican; if Blacks want a job, use the want ads because set asides are bad.

You poor black fool, you have fallen for the "okie doke" and that is real sad.

Wake up, man, you are being had. The white man is still in charge of the newspapers and the want ads.

There are set asides at Harvard, Princeton, and Yale for the white male, and there are set asides for black males in the county jail.

So, wake up, brother, because if you don't, there will be no one there when they come for you to go your bail.

Education

Mrs. Lillian Ryan Johnson, Woodard,
Aunt
(Courtesy of Mrs. Kathryn Eckert)

RUNNING OUT OF TIME

Rapping, twisting, and shaking your behind, but what are you doing to improve your mind?

Wake up, sisters and brothers; you are running out of time.

Education is a must; dancing and shaking is not enough. To succeed, studying, reading, and learning is the stuff. If you want to share in all the good things God has promised us.

Education

UNITE

You talk about your B.A., M.A., Ph.D. degrees. True education is a must, but the Klan, Nazis and skinheads are saying they are all n….rs to us.

You are not concerned when they are beating my head. Wake up! Can't you see tomorrow? They will be dragging you out of your bed, and filling you with lead.

So, if we unite, and support each other, we will all get ahead, – Instead of being dead.

JESUS AND BOOKS

Hey, come to the library with me.
Books are free and full of mystery; many wonderful things you will find to open your mind and void of crime.

The way to get ahead is to study, not sling lead.
There is a whole new world in books.
Try them; you might get hooked.
Forget about those crooks; our salvation is in Jesus and books.

Education

Mrs. Ivory Rochon Honoré. Cousin

BACK TO THE PAST

So, you are ashamed of spirituals, black poetry, blues, and jazz, and you say forget about slavery; it's in the past; we are riding first class.

Brothers and sisters, how long will we permit this foolishness to last?

History repeats itself, and if you don't get smart, Newt Gingrich, Phil Gramm, Clarence Thomas, and Bob Dole will kick your ass back to the past – fast!

ATTITUDE

Brothers and sisters, don't be fools;
stay in school,
obey the rules;
education – attitude should be your tool
because attitude determines your altitude, but
even if you fall, don't fret because the harder
you fall, the higher you will bounce, and you
will have no regrets.

EDUCATION IS THE WAY

Playing basketball all the time, but what are you doing to improve your mind?

Running up and down the court night and day; in school you should stay because education is the way.

Perfect your basketball skills,
for play, pay or thrills,
but get the education.
If basketball fails,
education will pay the bills.

Education

RUN MOVE

You are listening to Tupac Shakur and some of those other rapping fools.

Why don't you try and obey the rules and stay in school? Don't be a fool and have people use you as a tool.

The world is yours; reach out; grab it.
Run. Move!

Mrs. Dorothy Holmes Clark
(Courtesy of Mrs. Dorothy Clark)

REFLECTIONS

SAVE THE CHILDREN

If we had intervention and prevention, there would not be so much detention.

The wrongs are too numerous to mention.

Our children are dying every day and night without a fight.

Funeral homes are packed and have become horrible sights.

We are running out of patience; we must intervene, get their attention, so we can stop this devastation…and save this nation.

NO BED OF ROSES

We don't mind the rain... We don't mind the cold because we have heat coming from our hearts and souls.

We know life can be a storm, but a solid foundation will sustain us until the calm.

STAND UP, BE COUNTED

A people who do not love, respect, protect and have concern for each other cannot survive.

This lack of caring and neglect for each other will lead to our demise.

We must stop this madness. It behooves us all to get involved. It grieves and deeply saddens me to see the things that are happening to us.

Some of you are walking with your head held high, never looking from side to side, and you pretend you see nothing or you have buried your head in the sand. Wake up! Stand tall! This foolishness has a potential to do great harm to the Black man and destroy all of our plans.

Mrs. Lucille Davis

STRENGTH

My brothers, be cool: don't be a fool... You have nothing to prove... I know you want to take a hard stand and prove to the world you are a man, but why not have an alternate plan? Remember: "He who walks away will live to fight another day."

THE DEMISE OF THE POWERFUL

Oh! So, proudly you stand powerful man as you hold the keys to the world in your hand.

The sight of you, the sound of your voice causes men to tremble throughout the land. No one dares take position against you.

Ah, but all the power and wealth cannot shield you from what awaits. We inevitably have the same fate.

The paths of glory lead to the grave. No powers, accolades, or trophies will the tomb impart. No anthem to soothe or praise for the wicked heart.
On the headstone,

"HERE LIES THE DUST FOR THE WORMS TO SNORT."

MISGUIDED

Look at you walking with your head so high rain can fall in your nose. Your superior attitude shows.

You say we are not on your social economic level . . . and you think you are so clever . . . that ain't nothing but the devil.

You are no better than us. We all are walking to our demise so discard that disguise and join us because you too are nothing but dust.

Mrs. Stella "Mom" Breaux
(From Collection of Mrs. Matilda Redfud)

WORK

You say: "What's the
big deal?"
And I ask: "Why do you have to
rob and steal?
You can work to get a
meal."

VIOLENCE ON TV

People ask me: Why do you watch the violence on TV? And I say: Better I watch the violence on the TV than look out my window and have them shooting at me.

I'm afraid to go to the show to watch the violence, you know.

In your car, on the bus, or subway oftentimes it's a violent show.

So, I watch the violence on TV, and I feel safe, you see.

KINDRED SPIRITS

Why am I afraid of you, and why are you afraid of me?

Can't you see we are the same fruit from that big beautiful black tree?

CHRISTMAS IS

Christmas is Jesus, love, salvation, respect and praise coming from all nations, not shopping, fighting over toys, greed, and giving people things they don't want or need.

NO NAME

As a little child I lived in constant pain; what a shame. You see no one noticed me or cared about what I was or who I was. All the years of neglect, physical and mental pain kept me in a state of confusion and shame. I was constantly drained because Bastard and Sissy was my name!

No hugs, no kisses, no gentle touch, no sweet kind tender words and such.

All of my childhood was spent trying to ingratiate myself and please, but my only salvation was on my knees. Crying out to Jesus; asking that He would stand by me and see me through.

Only God knew my pain. I was His child even though to others, Bastard and Sissy was my name!

Mrs. Mary Hailey Harris, Cousin

SELF-ESTEEM

IT IS US AGAINST THE WORLD

It is indeed a good thing to love the peoples of the world, your country, your city, and your state and try to assimilate, but receiving hatred appears to be our fate.

So, remember: when you are Black, it does not matter how you act; you will constantly be under attack.

To counter these acts, let's fight back by learning to know, love, trust, respect, and protect each other.

Remember: no matter how brown, black or high yellow, that one drop of black blood makes us all sisters and brothers.

THE MASTER PLAN

Something happens to one white boy or girl and we are pulled from schools, taverns, off the streets; forced to take the DNA test; this is all a part of the master plan.

They will do anything but, treat you like a man. So our motto must be, "Divided we fall, together we stand."

We as a people cannot afford the luxury of being divided. Please let's make an effort to treat each other with, respect and dignity.

Remember to the Klan, skinheads, and Nazis, Bachelors, Masters or PhD, you are just another Black man, just like me.

If we are kind to each other, we can beat the odds and one day, we will all be free. And how sweet that will be.

THE DOPE FIEND SCROOGE

It was the night before Christmas
and there was not a thing in the house.

I had stolen and sold everything in the house.
Damn it! I'm a louse.

I got rid of the kid's presents and the Christmas tree.
For a bag of dope for no one but me.

I sat there in a daze, having those old dope fiend ways.

First it was the toys, and then the wife's fur coat.
Everything was going down like a sinking boat.

Something kept pushing me to smoke that cain
and it seemed I had no shame.

Self-Esteem

The minutes turned to hours, and the hours turned to days.

That's when I thought of blowing myself away to get out of this maze.

I raised the gun with my right hand. Suddenly I thought you are a better man than that. So, I grabbed my hat. I ran out of the house running, flying, like a bat. I didn't know where I was at.

I fell to my knees and said, "Oh Lord, I have no other hope but Thee."

I heard a voice saying, "It's time for recovery."

Now, I'm doing my steps one, two, and three, because my mother's prayers and my Christian up-bringing saved me.

STRONG, BEAUTIFUL AFRICAN AMERICAN WOMEN

Mrs. Mary Robinson Brown, Cousin

STOP! WAKE UP

Stop! Wake up, my brothers, sisters, fathers, mothers, families, neighbors, and friends. How long do you expect me to make amends? I am tired of hiding my sexuality. Just like you, I want to be free to live my life as it pleases me; so set me free. I am tired of this pain and misery.

You don't like what you see—too bad. I can't change; this is me. Accept it, or leave me be. I have got to be free!

TOO GOOD FOR DOPE

Look at me. Yes, look at me. I am Beautiful, Black, God-fearing, and Fine. Nothing! No alcohol, crack, coke or any other kind of dope is going to destroy my mind.

You see, God made me in His image, and I am too good for dope because it robs you of all hope. It will make you kill, rob, and steal.

Your mother, father, wife, sisters, brothers, friends – no one is exempt from the horrible things it will make you do.

Look in the mirror; tell yourself that you are the most important person in the world, and no dope is going to stop you. Tell yourself I've got plans: I am not going to put my future in the dope dealer's hands. Tell yourself no dope is going to ruin this beautiful body and mind or spoil my plans.

Self-Esteem

I am on my way to Yale, not jail. I am on my way to Morehouse, not the big house; to Penn State, not the state pen. I am going to the tennis court, not criminal court.

Yes, I am on my way to the sky, and I am so in love with me I get myself high. I don't need dope to get me high. Yes, I am too good for dope. I am not going to let the Man use me to complete his plan to destroy the Black man.

Why should I get 10 or 15 years for crack while rich men who use powdered coke get a pat on their backs? I am not going to jail for committing any vile acts to buy crack.

I am not going to let the man use me to create jobs for other people. Yes, all the prisons they are building for us mean we are improving the economy for other people. The corn fields, wheat fields, and even the desert are being used to house us.

Look around you and say to brothers and

sisters, "Not me."

I don't need dope to set me free from my pain and misery.

I am free because Jesus is in me. Yes, I am too good for dope; I don't want its pain and misery because Jesus is in me.

I am Black, Beautiful, and Free!

Self-Esteem

Mrs. Lucille Holmes Giles
(Courtesy of Mrs. Lucille Giles)

HAVE A PURPOSE

You sit at home and watch TV, constantly grumbling and complaining, "The whole world is against me."

You walk the streets drinking wine and using dope, talking about there is no hope… What a joke!

You won't even register and vote.

Straighten up; you can cope.

Too many people fought, suffered and died to pave a way for you.

Don't let them down.

Let's make their dreams come true.
It's the prudent thing to do.

BLACK GENOCIDE

My Black brothers, calm yourselves. You are going through the hood like a tornado destroying everything in your path.

Our seeds are not being allowed to grow. Our women's faces are beginning to resemble a waterfall from the tears running from their eyes.

How much longer must our mothers, fathers, brothers, sisters, family, and neighbors cry? Is it really necessary for so many of us to die?

Stop this madness, and replace this sadness with Black pride, love, respect and gladness.

HONOR

Once, God, honesty, integrity, and principle were Our Creed.

Now, it appears we are all filled with greed.

What has happened to pollute the beautiful black seed?

Wake up! How much longer must we bleed?

Self-Esteem

Mrs. Lucille Caroline Maura Holmes

THINK

So, you want to vote for the white man – and move back to the past?

You talk about the Black brother, saying we gonna kick that n....r's ass.

Wake up brothers and sisters; for the sickness you got, there is a cure.

Vote for the Black brother; stick together, and we shall be victorious. That's for sure.

SHAME

Hey, what is your name? Don't you have any shame?

Brother can't you see our sisters are tired of playing the crying game?

You are killing young boys and girls, and you don't even know their names.

You are causing our Black mothers and fathers great pain.

Hey! Don't you have any shame?

YOU THINK YOU'RE GREAT

You think you are great?
Why don't you walk tall, stand up straight.
Look at you sliding around like a snake.
Fix your hair; then people won't stare.
Be proud, cool, and still instead of wearing
baggy pants, hooded head – looking like the
poster boy for the Crime Bill.

BRING BACK SANITY

My Black brothers and sisters, bullets have no special address…

We are all a part of this mess,
and it is causing our people great distress.

No, most of us are not doing our best to confront these persons who are trying to destroy our communities and our children with these pervasive acts.

Let us come together and save our children and bring some love, purpose, respect and sanity back.

Ms. Aimee Olive Holmes

LOVE

Love and respect must be our creed.
When we love, we all succeed.

Let love replace hate and greed.
Yes, love is what we need today
in our work or in our play.

Love will make a brighter tomorrow and
replace sorrow.

When love leads our way,
trust and friendship will stay,
and many beautiful things will come our way.

Yes, love and respect must be our creed,
because without it, we cannot succeed.

LOVE AND RESPECT

If we are not concerned about each other – love, respect, and cherish our brothers, and honor our fathers and mothers – then some of us are destined to fail and languish in the gutter… or end up in jail.

TRY JESUS

Young Black men roaming the streets like mad dogs, killing each other like the slaughter house kills hogs.

The funeral homes have become assembly lines. Is this the sign of the times or is there something wrong with our minds?

Let's try Jesus again, and stop this mess. Following His teaching has always served us best.

Mrs. Alma Smyles Curtis "Ms Love"
(Courtesy of Ms. Doris Curtis)

WHAT DO WE NEED?

Jesus, love, and respect are the things we need to save our children from crime, hate, and greed.

So, let's acquire these with all deliberate spee

JESUS MY MOTIVATOR

In trying to reach my goals,
sometimes I am told,
"Move fast, you are getting old."
But, I am strong, bold,
a sight to behold.

However, there are times all the sacrifices I
made causes me to fret, and I appear to forget,
but my faith tells me yet…

Jesus is my inspiration,
the Ruler of all nations.
He is my foundation, salvation,
and my motivation.

With Him at my side,
I can ride the waves
and flow with the tide;
success cannot hide.

I am able to climb mountains, scale walls, leap
over all hurdles, fly with the eagles, and, like a

rocket, I can shoot to the sky.
No dream is too high.

Oh, how I fly with Jesus, my motivator, at my side!

STRONG, BEAUTIFUL AFRICAN AMERICAN WOMEN

Mrs. Debra Price-Ryan, Cousin
(From Collection of Charles Ryan, Sr)

FAMILY AGAIN

We must become a family again,
because families who love and respect
each other protect each other.

We must rise to the challenge before us,
because our survival depends on this.
No mountain is too high, with God's help.
Just like a rocket, we will shoot to the sky.

TOGETHERNESS

My Black sisters and brothers, we are like branches shooting out from the trunk of a large tree; we are heading in all directions, but we still have the same connection – the roots of that large tree.

None of us are free from each other, separate though we may be.

Remember one fungus can destroy the whole tree.

So, why not emulate the snowflakes, they are one of God's most fragile things, but look what they can do when they stick together.

SURVIVAL

Why are you always ready to attack?
I am not the one who has been riding your back.
Why can't we love and respect each other?
We are all sisters and brothers.
If we love each other and try to get along, we would be safe on the streets and in our homes.

Mrs. Amy Guidry Rochon, Aunt

MY OWN SALVATION

Why am I standing on the street corner, my mind full of wine, dope and no hope?
This has to be a joke.
How did I get to this point?

What has happened to my dreams?
I am lost.
I used to be clean, suave and lean.
There is no gleam, only darkness it seems. I guess I'll have to change this scene and reclaim my dreams.

A HOUSE DIVIDED

A house divided against itself cannot stand.

Wake up brother man;
our goal is the Promise Land.

Can't you see by robbing, stealing, killing you are helping the Klan?

Our great brains and talents are in demand.

Wake up, brother man, education and love is our ticket to the Promise Land.

Can't you see a house divided against itself cannot stand?

Self-Esteem

MY NEIGHBORHOOD

Boys of the Hood: that's what we call the dudes in my neighborhood.

Most of us would leave if we could.
I really think all of us should.
Our future looks dim;
we are hemmed in.
We are searching, begging for help and love.

It appears we can't even get intervention from above.
Where will all this end?   If someone doesn't help us fend from this madness we are in, we will never become men.

Brothers and sisters who have made it, you have played it well.

Please, come back and help to save us from this living hell, or there will be a sad story to tell about you and the Boys in the Hood, as well.

DR. KING

Rev. Dr. Martin Luther King was a rare human being, a man supreme. He had a dream; he was clean and of meager means, and yet, it seems in his God he did trust and he did all he could for us.

No more sitting on the back of the bus. And at lunch counters, we can sit without a fuss.

How he was criticized and despised and sometimes ostracized!
What a surprise when he died,
and the whole world cried.

If he could come back today and open his eyes, he would be surprised to see so many young black men and women in their demise.

Some won't even try. Come out. If we walk hand-in-hand together, we can reach the sky. Keep his dream alive.

Self-Esteem

Mrs. Shirley Button Holmes

INTOLERANCE

BE KIND

It sounds like an old cliché when we hear people say, "No man is an island, and we all need someone or each other."

So, why is it so hard to give people the time of day?

When we walk out of our homes or walk down the street, wouldn't it be just great if we would greet and say, "Hello" to people we meet?

Even if a person doesn't have a dime, it does not cost anything to smile and give them a kind look or a moment of time.

Remember: Jesus is saying, "You are still all mine".

IS THIS TRUE?

They say a Black man ain't shit.

Is this true?

Here are some of the things that they say he will do.
He'll screw your wife and your daughter too.
And if you don't watch him, he'll try to screw you.
He'll cut your throat and go to jail.
Then ask your wife to go his bail.
He'll sit in jail hoping you die.
But when he gets before the judge, he'll begin to cry.
He'll raise hell in the hood both day and night, but if you mention going to the white hood, he is filled with fright.

He will not listen to Black men or women when they try and tell him what's right.
But in jail and prison, he is a sorry sight.
When the white guards tell him when he can

eat, shower, play and go to bed at night.

But there is one thing he can't do, and that's tell you where he's going to get a job, be responsible, start life anew, pay you and all his other bills that are past due.

Is this really true?

Ms. Earnestine Ann Porter

BLACK FACE

You put a Black face on crime.
Are you out of your mind?

You put a Black face on welfare,
as if we care;
white folks are getting more than their share.

Can't you see the jails and prisons in Europe,
Asia, and the Far East are filled – and not with
me?

You put a Black face on rape; that's nothing but
hate because these white boys are killing and
raping in every city and state.

Let's go back to the past.
You were busy watching me; that's why you
couldn't see those Japanese coming to bomb
your ass.

Intolerance

How long will this last?
Keep watching me, and we will all go down like the ships on the bottom of the sea. BE KIND.

It sounds like an old cliché when we hear people say, "No man is an island, and we all need someone or each other."So, why is it so hard to give people the time of day?

When we walk out of our homes or walk down the street, wouldn't it be just great if we would greet and say, "Hello" to people we meet?

Even if a person doesn't have a dime, it does not cost anything to smile and give them a kind look or a moment of time.

Remember: Jesus is saying you are all mine.

JUST TO FEEL FREE

To live as a man and be truly free appears to forever elude me.

My only escape is to bury me head in the proverbial sand and live in constant denial.

How wonderful it would be for me, if we could for just one day, walk the streets and really feel free.

But how can it be when I get the looks, the frequent police stops and no matter how inconspicuous I am they still notice me.

Once I was called the invisible man, but now everyone sees me.

Oh, just for once too truly feel and be free.

Intolerance

THE MASON

Our Black Brothers served in the Navy on the big battle ship the Mason.

Oh Lord, how they tried to help the nation. Through the storms and high waves they rode, and sometimes in the icy waters they dove.

German subs they did sink, and still they got no thanks.

In London, England when they arrived; a hot dog, and a coke was all they desired. They were told no Blacks inside; we, too, practice Jim Crow with pride. Only when they got to Ireland, did they find there was no fuss and no Jim Crow to raise its head and embarrass us.

V. E. Day came and still nobody mentioned their names.

Lord does this nation have no shame?

For thirty-eight years we were ignored, until a great man came aboard and with good intentions, this great man, whose name is President Clinton, gave us an honorable mention.

Now we can go to Annapolis, a place from which they kept us, and see young Black men and women graduating with honors and distinctions.

Thank God. Never again will they be pushed in a corner and deprived of honor.

Intolerance

Ms. Stella Mae Breaux
(From Collection Mrs. Matilda Redfud)

THEY DIDN'T GET TO KNOW ME

I did all the things I should.
I worked as hard as I could.
I played by the rules even when
I was called a fool.

But, it was all for naught, for there were things
I could not change. No, it was not my name,
but it causes me great pain.

What a shame: before they got to know me,
they saw me.

GOD'S CHILDREN

We are all God's children and striving to be free, so why should Cubans, Asians, Eastern Europeans and Hispanics have preference over Haitians and people like me, when it comes time to be accepted in my country, America, the home for those who want to be free?

Everyone else is accepted in this homeland of the free, but Africans, Haitians, and other Blacks like me, who are left to drown and be food for the fishes in the bottom of the sea.

UNHONORED

Other peoples' rights we fought so hard and honorable to protect and all we got was neglect.

We fought to protect the settlers on the plains and they did not care about knowing our names.

We fought in the war between the states, still all we got was hate.

The Spanish American War we did too, though our accolades were few.

World War One they thought was a breeze, until those Germans almost had them on their knees and they said, "Oh brothers, would you please!"

World War II we did great, but they refused to desegregate.

Intolerance

The Korean War we were in, but, falling in those honey buckets was a sin.

Vietnam we did fine, but, many of us lost our minds and when we returned they treated us like we had committed a crime.

The Gulf War we did make to free Kuwait.

In all these wars our contributions we did make, and we did not hesitate.

A Purple Heart they gave me, but still I am not free.

The people I fought come to my country and are treated better than me.

STRONG, BEAUTIFUL AFRICAN AMERICAN WOMEN

Mrs. Idella Gray Landry

Intolerance

DON'T BLAME ME

So, you blaming me for what I be, but, who
was there to save me from what I have become.

I have no feeling; I am numb; you would be
too, if you came from the same place as me.

Where all I see is gangs, dope pushers, dealers,
robbers, users, so don't blame me, when all I
see is killings, welfare and no workfare and
nobody gives a care about little old me.

The apple does not fall too far from the tree.
I did not fall. I was chopped down at the knee.

So don't blame me for what you see.
Cause if I had your mama or papa to care
about me and could have shared in your
happiness, a different person I'd be.
I would still be a bright fine apple in that tree.

THE TRUTH WILL SET YOU FREE

It is said the truth will set you free, and I ask, "How can it be, when I have always dealt in truth, but it does not help me?"

Because black and not truth, is seen when people look at me.

WE ARE IN THIS TOGETHER

In the cities or suburbs, no matter where you live; it's a fact, thieves, whores, punks, educators, conservative Republicans or Democrats, it doesn't matter: if you are Black, we are all treated alike.
Because the only thing they see is Black.

NORTH OF THE MASON DIXON LINE

I left the lazy laughing South with blood on its mouth and came North just in time to find there were still "colored" and "members only" signs. No real promised land I found, but more racism and boundaries north of the Mason Dixon line.

They said to me, "Give it time;
you'll get yours like I got mine."
Man, I didn't have a dime.
Still, I worked and saved
and did progress
in spite of this mess.
Now, I'm put through another test.
Damn! Will I ever get any rest?

OTHER

So, you say you are not Black;
you want to be called other.
That's not going to get you any further,
Brother.
They are still going to hold on to their purses,
refuse to ride you in cabs,
lock their doors, and
follow you in the stores, and
treat our women like whores.

Mrs. Elaine Wiltz Holmes
(Courtesy of Mrs. Elaine Holmes)

PRAYER

TRY PRAYER

You say you don't want prayer in school, and forget about the Golden Rule.

Wake up! Don't be fooled and allow yourself to be somebody's tool.

Think back in time…Prayer gave us a conscious, clean mind, and it kept us in line. Even when we didn't have a dime, our faith let us know that things would be just fine.

So, let's try prayer again instead of dope because without it, there is no hope.

Let us not be fools; let us love each other and practice the Golden Rule.

Prayer

OUR SURVIVAL IS IN THEE

Dear God, I am down on bended knee with head high looking up and around to Thee, asking you to please send Jesus to touch and come into our hearts, and set my people free. We have tried dope, alcohol, and nothing at all can replace Your call.

Lord, sometimes we cry when we walk or drive down the streets and see so many of our young people in their demise, and no matter how much we talk, plead, and cajole, we cannot get their attention. If we do not surmount this problem, the consequences are too numerous to mention.

Lord, our eyes have become blind; we cannot see how wonderful and beautiful we are when we put our faith in Thee.

All I see is people going to the gambling boats, and the betting parlors. What has happened to the revivals, prayer meetings, and the beautiful greeting: Praise the Lord, God bless you, and pray for me?

Lord, please help my people see that our survival is in Thee. As I bow on bended knee, please, Lord, look down on my people, and set them free, and help them to realize that all really good things come from Thee,
and we will never be free until every one of us treats each other with respect and dignity.

Help us to see we are destroying our own precious babies and children, and our women and seniors are afraid and filled with pain and misery, and it is all because we have turned from Thee.

Touch our hearts, our minds; please help us stop these crimes. In Jesus' name we ask Thee: Please help us and set us free, and bring us closer to Thee.
Amen.

Prayer

WILL IT EVER END?

Sometimes it appears that all of the beautiful things in life have blown out to sea, and the waves bring back to us nothing but debris and misery.

Nobody sings, whistles, speaks or smiles anymore.

It seems our hearts are hard and rotten to the core.

We are in our homes behind locked doors and can't sit on our porches anymore.

Oh, God! Will things ever be as they were before?

STRONG, BEAUTIFUL AFRICAN AMERICAN WOMEN

Ladies of Lake Charles

Front Row Left to right: Mrs. "Sugar Doo", Mrs. Amy Guidry Rochon, Mrs. Givens, Mrs. Alma Smyles Curtis
Back Row: Mrs. Barkay, Mrs. Haley, ?, ?

HELP

Help! Why can't I stop this cycle that I am in?
I have wronged my family and even my best friend.

My dreams are haunted by things from my past.
I awake grabbing my head saying, "How long can this last?"

The wrongs that I have done are more than a few.
Those ghosts are around every corner waiting to say, "Boo!"

Somehow I must make amends to my family and friends.

Then, with God's help, I can make this nightmare end.

LOOKING FOR A SMILE

Why is it so hard to get a smile, kind word, or look from my Black sisters and brothers?

I can understand it when I am mistreated by others.

But, dear God, why am I so wronged and misunderstood by my own Black sisters and brothers?

Can't you see; I am you and you are me? We are all swimming in this big Black Sea.

Prayer

FAITH

Oh, Lord! What did we do to deserve this end when our only sin is the color of our skin?

We have served and praised you from way back when. Please look down on our children, and save them as you did Daniel in the lion's den.

Save our children from a tragic end.

JESUS IS NEAR

Sometimes it feels like we are insects
trapped in ancient stone—but remember
Our Lord is still on the throne.
He will never leave you alone,
He always watches over and takes care of His own.

With this faith we can persevere.
So never fear, Jesus is always near.
Therefore remember you are not like the insect in the stone, because you are cradled in Jesus' arms.

Prayer

COME TOGETHER

I am young, gifted, and wise, but my greatest fear is will I survive when all around me I see Black genocide.
Brothers being killed not by the Klan, but by another black man's hand.

Let's come together and take a stand; this foolishness is spoiling all of our plans. Black women can't walk the streets; our babies – being raped and shot in their sleep...

Oh, God! Help us before we are all six feet deep.
And before our time, we meet at Jesus' feet.

Mrs. Susie Williams Castille

MONOLOGUES

AMERICA, I LOVE YOU!

When the merciless sun was beating down my back and my head felt as if it would crack, and the tears I held back, because,
America, I love you!

When my arms ached, and my fingers and hands are filled with blisters, my chest feels like it is ready for a heart attack,
America, I love you!

Washing and ironing your clothes, cooking on a wood stove. And after you and your family would dine, you'd make me take my food outdoors to sit on the steps to eat.

America, I love you!

You hang my sons, husbands and brothers from a tree… And you have just gotten out of bed caressing and making love to me.
America, I love you!

I nursed your children, loved them as my own, and before they were grown, I had to call them Mr. or Miss. I had to neglect my own to cook and clean your home.
America, I love you!

I cooked your food, baked your bread, put my hands on and in everything you ate.
I did it with love, not hate;
still, you made me use the back gate.
America, I love you!

Like an unwanted child begging to be loved, I tried to please,
I did everything but get on my knees and beg, oh massa, please!

I wanted to serve in all of your wars; open the gates, and let me in.
I am your friend.
America, I love you!

December the seventh, nineteen hundred and forty-one was said to be a day of infamy because the Japanese had attacked us without warning.

We as a people of color worked and fought as hard as most and harder than some. Yet, you treated German prisoners of war better than you treated me. They could eat in white restaurants while being transported to other bases, but you refused to serve black GI's who had been wounded in combat. Black entertainers, had to entertain German prisoners of war before they entertained Black GI's. And after the war was over, American dollars were poured into Japan and Europe to rebuild them. The Emperor of Japan came to America and was treated better than me.

America, I love you!

You refused to let me fight in your wars until Mrs. Eleanor Roosevelt and President Harry S Truman said remove all barriers; this has to end. You had nightclubs in my neighborhood with Black entertainers and you would not let me in. However,
America, I love you!

You refuse to ride me in your cabs.
You follow me in stores.
When you see me coming, you lock your car doors.
America, I love you!

You refuse to give me construction jobs. When I walk or drive down the street, I see other men and women working, but I don't see me.
America, I love you!

You won't give me the jobs and don't want me on welfare.

America, I love you!

You make heroes of all your criminals: the James Boys, Baby Face Nelson, Butch Cassidy, Ma Barker, John Dillinger, Al Capone and other Mafia persons; you make sympathetic movies about them – even have museums honoring them.

They could have killed thousands of people, but you will still welcome them in your neighborhood. But, no matter what my accomplishments, I am still unwelcome.

You afforded me the worst education. Many times it was in a one or two room shack. You would even take me out of school and force me to put a cotton sack on my back.

You gave me an inferior education and then asked, "Why can't you excel like other immigrants in this nation?" You forget they were allowed to assimilate and to go to school with you.

I could not talk back to you. If I did, I was beaten, jailed, lynched, or all of the above. So, I took out my frustration on my wife, children, and other Blacks that I loved.

If I killed a Black man or woman, the penalty was not as severe. You would go to the authorities and tell them that Boy is my best field hand or my best waiter, houseboy. I need him to do my work, and more times than not, I would be set free.

Even today my life is not valued as much as others. Some people get more time for killing a dog than for killing me.

You go to Church, you pray, you say you love the Lord. But, he can't get you to love and respect me.
I see, it is really a mystery to me.

Stepchild, second-class citizen, that I may be, but you are still the greatest country in the world to me.

My blood, sweat, and tears are in your soil.
My music is in your ears.
My dance movements are in your steps.

I cut your sugar cane.
I harvest your crops.
I made cotton king.
I built your castles and plowed in the rain.
You treat your dogs, cats, and other animals such as monkeys and gorillas better than you treat me.

You will hug and kiss them for the whole world to see, but you refuse to touch me.
America, I love you!

All of my life you have done to me what a baby does to a diaper, but America, I shall always love you.

Don't deny me, America!
No one has loved you as much as I.
No one has loved you as much as I
Don't deny me, America, I love you!

Mrs. Ruth Dixon

THE BENCH

Hey! I'm Richard! You don't know me, but I'm Richard . . . I know you've seen me before. I sit right here every day God sends and just watch the world go by. I see you just about every morning driving by in your fancy car lookin' straight ahead like I wasn't here. I used to wave at you when you looked at me once in a while. But then you turned up your nose and looked the other way. And I said to hell with you, Buster. And I never waved no more.

Folks are something else! Sometimes they walk by and I can hear'em say things like: "Oh, chil', that clown's either on dope or the bottle! Look at his eyes." They act like I can't hear what they say, but I can. Sometimes I want to answer 'em and say, "I ain't about to poison my system with no drugs or no booze." And besides in my financial condition, I can't afford the luxury of either one. Just getting food to eat once in a while is hard enough . . .

I used to be somebody! I use to wear a coat and tie and carry a briefcase and be "MISTER" Richard N. Smith! Had me a really nice job. Made over thirty thousand a year. Reagan was president then, and he was crowin' about how good things were. Talking about how he had put the world to work. And, like while he was saying it, the company I worked for laid me off! Can you believe that? The whole wide world was put back to work, the President said, but me and a bunch of folks I worked with were being placed on permanent layoff. And I'll be damned. If I didn't look around and found my neighbor had been laid off; another guy down the block and a guy who lived behind me also got the axe about the same time. I decided I'd drop the President a line to let him know somebody was making a liar out of him. I told him what was going on in my neighborhood. And asked him if he would kindly tell me where all them folks he was talking about had found their jobs, so me and the folks on my block could find some, too. Of course, he didn't send me no answer . . .

Anyway, I was somebody once. I had a wife, a house, and two kids. Back in '75, I spent a month in the hospital on account of my diabetes. Guess between that and high blood pressure and being poor as the devil, ain't a whole lot left. So I get up every morning I can and come down here and sit on this old bench and watch the world go by...

You see a whole lotta things out here. Whole lotta things! Hear a lot of things, too. See that turkey standing over there by that store? He ain't up to no good. He's a coke head – and I don't mean Coca-Cola. Pop pills, too, when he can get'em. Right now, he's looking to make a buy. He's got to have that junk. His brain's already messed up, but he keeps on frying them. If somebody don't kill him, he's gonna wake up dead from all that junk he's putting in his body. Course I'll give him credit; he ain't never messed with me. He thinks I'm crazy. Well, what do you expect? I told you his brains was fried.

Good morning, ma'am. How are you today?

Lovely day aint it? Oh I just fine, just fine thank you. Now that's a nice lady, always has a pleasant good mornin'. Christian woman, too. One day she stopped and asked me if I had had anything to eat. I lied and told her my stomach was full as a tick. And she just patted my hand and said, "God loves you." The way she said it, sent a little tingle straight through me. Yes sir, she is a good woman.

Ain't nothing like that one over there. That one's a pickpocket when she ain't prostituting. She's over there standing at the bus stop like she's on her way somewhere. I'm talking about the woman with the black coat hanging on her shoulders. Look at her. Look at her pushing up behind that well dressed gentleman with the briefcase in one hand, a notebook in the other. See? She stuck with him until he got on the bus, now she's stepping back. That turkey's been plucked as sure as you're born. And she's gonna keep plucking right up 'til the rush hour is over. Then she'll start her other business...Reckon business must be good; she drives a brand new BMW.

And everybody says she paid cash for it. I spoke to her one time, and that put her nose out of joint. She screwed that prune face of hers up and said, "Don't be messing with me! I'm a business woman and you ain't hardly in my league!" If I hadn't been a gentleman, I'd have told her where to kiss; and probably would have ended the invitation with the word that means the same a female dog. But I try so hard to be a gentleman.

Here comes the young professor. He told somebody he was a sociologist down at one of the colleges. He told this guy he finds me interesting. Now he can't be that dumb. Even I know that sociology is the study of society – and I ain't hardly no society. Look at how close he's standing! Now he ain't gonna get to close. He don't want me to know he's trying to hear anything I might say. Well, I may as well make his day. When mama stabbed daddy with the pretty scissors; daddy's blood flew out. And that's when we knew who we were! I remember mama crying out, "Your daddy's a blue blood!" Look at his eyes buck! Now watch this. I got to go to the bathroom so bad! Is that a tree standing over there near my bench? It's got two – what's them? – trunks, I do believe. Maybe I'll stand behind it and relieve myself. Umph! Them trunks look like they're wearing shoes! Did you ever see anybody run so fast in your life? Now he'll make a big to-do about me. Probably tell his students how society has crushed me; and made me crazy and a whole lotta other bull crap. But that's alright. Maybe I am a little bit crazy. Maybe we're all a little bit crazy. I don't know. I don't know…

Truth is, maybe I spend too much time thinking – too much time thinking about what I could have been, or who I could have been? Too much time feeling sorry for myself. Somewhere out there I got two kids; I haven't seen since their mama walked out on me, back in '75. They're my own flesh and blood. The boy would be close to thirty-two and the girl would be around thirty. They don't know if I'm living or dead. Now, ain't that a cause of the Hallelujah Chorus! – But that's alright. The sun still rises in the East and sets in the West; I try not to think too much about it. But I got to be honest with you; it gets me right here where I live. The old lady and I were happy together for a long time. I mean we were family in the real sense of the word. Maybe I wanted too much for them. I don't know. I took a second job to help us get some of the extra things I thought we ought to have – to help make ends meet. Later, I learned that it wasn't just the ends that were meeting. My wife was meeting another guy. And then when I lost the second job, I could sense that she was changing. At least she was honest about it. She came to me, and said, "Rich, I got to tell you something." Even before she said it, I knew. A thing like that's easy to know. You don't want to admit it but you know a long time before you are told. She said I was a nice person. She didn't want to hurt me, but she had met another guy and they were in love. I don't think I said a word. My eyes got so blurred that I couldn't see a thing. And my chest got so numb, it was like I died. And I reckon in a way I did. That was the first time I ever felt that kind of pain. The next day, I moved out . . . I signed some papers. She sold the house and I never saw or heard of her or my kids again. Somebody said they moved to another town . . . But, hey, nobody said life would be easy or fair. You take the cards you are dealt and play your hand. And that's all you can do when you get right down to it . . . I learned a long time ago that folks spend too much time pretending to be what they ain't. And trying to convince themselves that they can be what they can't. I got no time for put-ons and show-offs! First place; they ain't fooling nobody but themselves. Acting like they weren't born like everybody else – like they are immaculate conceptions – and we know only Christ was considered to be an immaculate conception! But, some folks go around with their nose stuck up in the air like they smelling something somebody did by mistake; and they think they're the reason the sun rises. And don't you tell them no different. I always want to walk up to folks like that and say to them right square off, you going to die like everybody else! That's the equalizer. And the same worms that are going to eat my ass are going to eat yours. I hear folks say, "Old so'n so was born to make money" if a guy's got a hold of a few bucks in his life. Or somebody else "was born" to do this or that. Damn lie! Nobody – and I don't care who he is – was born to do nothing but die! Now cold as it sounds, that's a fact.

And that brings me to another thing, how come we make such a big to-do when somebody dies? We really start dying the day we are born – and we get a little practice in every time we go to sleep. Oh, yeah. And then one day when we've got it down right, we just go into it permanently! Like I said, what do I know? That's just my opinion. I wouldn't want folks interrupting their lives to ritualize my death. It won't bring me back, and I don't believe I'll know a damned thing about it. So who's the show for? Just let a crematorium do his number; and ask somebody to send an announcement to people I knew saying, "Old Crazy Richard finally got dying right. And 'cause he wasn't taken with the idea of being shut up in a coffin and laying in a hole in the ground. His wish to be cremated was honored; and his ashes were scattered to the winds. He wanted you to know and he asks that you go on with your lives." Simple and to the point... Anyhow, that's what I think. Sorry I brought the subject up – No, I'm not really!

Well, I see the old coke head is heading back this way. He musta made a connection. Look at that walk would you? He's just bouncing and dipping and pulling that left arm behind him like he's fanning flies off his butt. What in the world? I guess that's what you'd have to call being cool. Now I reckon that's an example of a dap walk. Dap! Dap! Dap! If he got any cooler than that, by God, he'd snow! Here he comes. Here he comes. Now watch him! Watch him. Humph! My God, he's flying without an airplane! Fried brain dummy!

Monologues

The Bench

STRONG, BEAUTIFUL AFRICAN AMERICAN WOMEN

Mrs. Beatrice Lafleur Guidry, Aunt
(Courtesy of Mrs. Lilly Brazil)

GOD'S JUDGMENT OR MAN PLAYING GOD?

There is a Balm in Gilead,
To make the wounded whole.
There is a Balm in Gilead,
to heal the sin sick soul...

You know, I had been married ten years and had me two daughters; I loved them very much, but I always wanted me a son.

Then praise God. One day my wife tells me she's pregnant. Well, don't you know I was just praying for me a boy. And bless the Lord. Wouldn't you know it? I had me a boy. Look out pro football, baseball, and basketball. Here comes my son!
When he was about eight, I started him in the Little League. But, I could see he was not interested. However, I continued to push him. He played for about four years, then he wouldn't play anymore; I had to accept that.

I noticed he had this thing for hair. He was always trying to play with his mother's and sister's hair.

As he grew older, he started talking about being a beautician. I sure didn't want to see any son of mine as any hairdresser. I wanted him to be a scientist, an engineer, a lawyer, a doctor, a football, a basketball, or a baseball player. Well, he became a hairdresser – a beautician – and people were talking about how good he was. The women were just going crazy over his work. He opened his own shop, and he shot straight to the top. Everyone said they were proud of him. That is, except me. I said to my friends, "Everyone has a son, and I have a beautician." I was hurt and ashamed of my son, so I kept my distance.

He eventually got his own apartment; everything was going great – for a while. Then I noticed he began to look different. He was losing weight. He moved back home and began to go to church with his mother all the time, and he started praying for everybody. Then he got pneumonia, and the doctors told us he had the virus they call – you know this thing some of these preaches are calling God's raft on homosexuals for their sins: their life style. I didn't worry about the weight loss. I figured once he started eating his mother's good greens, sweet potatoes, beans, rice, potato salad, peach cobbler, and sweet potato pies, he would be just fine. Well, the weight loss continued, then he got pneumonia. We kept our faith, and we continued to believe in the Word, and he rallied back.

Now, I have always been a God-fearing man… I don't know about you, but I don't understand a God who is going to hurt homosexuals and do nothing to these crooked politicians and world leaders who are responsible for thousands of people starving and dying, and don't mention the ministers who are whoremongers, robbers, and vipers. What about the dope dealers, pushers, skinheads, Nazis, Klan members, and all of the gang members? Nobody is bothering them; even the authorities can't do anything to stop them. So, why homosexuals? If you say they are sinning, is this the only sin? Who are they hurting?

You know what I think? I think man had something to do with this virus. It was created in a laboratory – think about it.

My son was always a good, decent, God-fearing young man as are his friends. So, why would God infect them and let all of these murders and other ungodly people go free.

Well, my son continued to improve, and then he had a relapse, and from then on, it was downhill. Then... one morning his mother went into his room, and his spirit had left him.

Now, I think about all the times my son

reached out to me, and I stepped back. It's whipping the hell out of me. I think about all the times I called young boys who were effeminate sissies, faggots, and queers.

I guess what I am saying is – be careful of what you say about people because when you have children, you can't talk about other peoples' children: You never know what is going to visit your family.

Son, daddy loved you, and he misses you. Oh, God! How he misses you! I loved you with all my heart; I just didn't know how to show you. I promise you, Son, as God is my witness, I'm going to do everything in my power to work and help find a cure for this virus.

> *Sometimes I feel discouraged,*
> *And think my work's in vain,*
> *But then the Holy Spirit,*
> *Revives my soul again...*

Ms. Elizabeth Cecelia Porter

I AM MAD AS CAN BE

Yes, I am mad as can be, because they raped our grandmothers in the outhouses, big houses and fields, and bastards they made us be. Now we hear all this talk about being *multi-racial* and *other*. Do you really believe, sisters and brothers, that is going to get us any further?

Everybody talking about Tiger Woods. Now I love the brother but, look at other so called Blacks. Some of us have Irish-blood, Japanese-blood, Italian-blood, French-blood, Polish-blood, English-blood, Asian-blood, East Indian-blood and Lord don't forget Native American Indian-blood and still they avoid us like they do a puddle of mud! Now people are worried about mixed race children—they weren't worried about mixed race children when they were raping our women! This thing really upsets me—mulatto, high yellow, light skinned, and coffee & cream. We are still treated mean. We can't get a cab; they follow us in stores; and they treat our women as if they were whores; and when they see us coming, they lock their car doors.

When the police stop me, what am I going to say? Can I say, "Oh officer look at me; I am an *other*? I am *multi-racial*. My grandmother came from Ireland too. So officer what are you going to do?"

You know you hear the white folks say in their family there is Indian, Irish, Scott, English, French, but do you ever hear any of them saying they got black blood? Why not?

Let me tell you something; when you are in the supermarket, the mall, restaurant, baseball, basketball or football games, just keep your eyes opened and look around you.

You will see more so-called white folks with kinky hair, big lips, broad features and wide noses—can't you see Uncle Tom has been there? Yes indeed; they are white and don't you tell them any different. But for us, it does not matter what kind of blood we have; we are all the same to them, n....rs! It does matter how you see yourself, or what you say or think you are. It is how white folks see you. If they see some black features, then you are Black and it does not matter how you act.

Let me tell you all something; all of this *other* and mixed race stuff is just some more shit to keep us divided!

So, just remember; no matter how Black, brown, white, or high yellow you are, that one-drop makes us all sisters and brothers!

Mrs. Ella Rougeau Lafleur
(Courtesy of Mrs. Lilly Brazil)

ALL WE HAVE LOST AND WHERE DID IT GO?

There was a time when mother, country, flag, National Anthem and patriotism were the things that made America great and us a wonderful people. I should also add respect, honor, duty integrity, responsibility, principle and please don't forget dignity, manners and pride.

The days when people were kind, considerate, understanding, thoughtful and giving! Where did they go? These are things we held dear and appear to have lost, where did they go? We were family; children did not have to be paid to do things in and around the home or to earn good grades or take care of their younger siblings.

The days when mothers, women and older people were respected and revered. Where did they go?

There was a time when father knew best and mother was the greatest and her love, understanding, advice, wisdom and cooking was better than all the rest. Where did they go?

Now we see comics and television shows portraying fathers as idiots and the children with wisdom and they know best. Once we had romance and love—now everything is sex. Back-in-the-day, not only were girls virgins, boys were too.

Back-in-the-day, people had manners; they respected each other and authority. Neighbors, parents, teachers, administrators, ministers, priest rabbis and police got the utmost respect. If parents were not home, neighbors could control children. If there was a disturbance, the National Anthem would be played and things would come to order.

Ladies could walk the streets without fear;

there were no muggers, purse snatchers, rapist, or carjackers, but a gentleman was always near to pull back a chair, open a door, take off his hat, extend his arm and escort ladies there. Chivalry is not dead; it is just not being demanded. Gentlemen did not sit with ladies with their hats on in restaurants.

There were no metal detectors, policemen or security guards in our schools. For the most part, we all adhered to the rules. Jails and prisons were not one of the largest industries. When a person gave you their word, you could count on it; because your word was your bond. A handshake could seal a deal. Dear God, how did we lose it and where did it go?

Will we ever start teaching love, manners and instilling principle, integrity, respect, manners and honor in our children again?

In conclusion there is still hope. We can return to the ethos that made us a great and wonderful people.

Dear God, I hope so. Because a people who do not love, respect and treat each other with dignity are in for some perilous times.

Keep your eyes open and look around you my friends. As the old Black ladies would say, "The handwriting is on the wall. A hint to the wise is sufficient!" Remember we are all branches on that large tree and swimming in that Beautiful Black Sea. I am no better than you and you are no better than me; we are all God's children, don't you see. And remember, "We are all born between urine and feces and destined to become a delectable delight for the terrestrial earthworms." And the heavenly Secretary is recording everything we do. From the day we are born until the day we die, everything in-between is our dash and only what we do for Christ will last.

Jesus, love, education, pride, honor, support,

dignity, respect, caring and manners are the things we need to save the beautiful Black seed.

Remember, a snowflake is the most fragile thing God has made, but Lord, look what happens when they stick together? PRESIDENT OBAMA!

Love and God Bless!
Melvin C. Ryan

www.ingramcontent.com/pod-product-compliance
Lightning Source LLC
Chambersburg PA
CBHW022104090426
42743CB00008B/708